ישראל

ISRAEL

ישראל

ISRAEL

The Blessing The Church Does Not Want

Ray A. Beattie

authorHOUSE®

AuthorHouse™ UK Ltd.
1663 Liberty Drive
Bloomington, IN 47403 USA
www.authorhouse.co.uk
Phone: 0800.197.4150

Published by AuthorHouse   05/16/2013

ISBN: 978-1-4817-9602-6 (sc)
ISBN: 978-1-4817-9603-3 (e)

CONTENTS

Introduction vii

Chapter 1   Can we depend on God's promises? ... 1

Chapter 2   What is so special about God's
             promises to Abraham? 7

Chapter 3   Why Israel? 23

Chapter 4   What has this old covenant got to do
             with me as we have a new one? 35

Chapter 5   The Palestine problem 39

Chapter 6   What is Israel's future? 49

Chapter 7   Blessings or Curses? 57

INTRODUCTION

The nation of Israel is tiny by any standards. You can drive from one end to the other easily within a day and yet despite its size it is always in the news. It is a nation which polarises opinions. Jewish folk and Arabs both vie for possession of the land and recent history has been one of bitter conflict and seemingly there is no answer to this vexing problem. The Jewish nation has experienced dreadful atrocities perpetrated against it and in 1948 established itself as a recognised state in the land. This immediately led to wars and conflicts as the Arab residents did not recognise the new state of Israel.

As Christians we recognise that the gospel of Jesus Christ is for all no matter what their ethnicity and our love should be toward all men because Christ has loved us in equal measure. How then can we square the circle? What should our view be toward the Jew and Arab? What has God's word to say about this situation if anything?

If you are confused or not sure where you stand in relation to this issue it is my hope that this book will clarify your thoughts. Scripture has a lot to say about our attitude in this matter and I want to take you through it. Put aside all your preconceived ideas and quietly reflect on what the word says.

It is my earnest desire that the Lord will speak to you as you meditate and spend time with Him.

CHAPTER 1

Can we depend on God's promises?

It seems a long time ago, I recall, that as a family we sat around the tea table on a Sunday afternoon and before we ate we took turns to extract a promise with tweezers from the promise box. It became a ritual which as children we enjoyed, not so much for the biblical promises, but for the fascination of taking out a tightly rolled scroll, reading it aloud, and then putting it back the other way up so that a red colour was visible thus showing which of the scrolls had been read. It was the time following the Second World War and certain items of food were still rationed. For all this, families pulled together and were probably closer units than at the present time and although as children we did not appreciate it, available funds had to be wisely spent. The family rule at tea was jam on every second piece of bread. On one occasion there was a disagreement between my brother and me because we both reckoned that it was our turn to take out the promise. The promise box was grasped by both of us and so began a tug of war. Neither of us won however as the box was released quickly by one of the hands and ended upside down on the table amongst the food. The promises spilled out and before salvaging them all and restoring them in some order to the box, we received another promise from our father. It was a promise that we did not want to hear!

As believers in the Lord Jesus Christ we are recipients of many promises from our heavenly father. Some have become very precious to us and we have proved them to be so real in our own experience. It would be unthinkable to consider that God would renege on any of his promises and yet, sadly, this is exactly what a section of the Church believes. There is a promise the Church just does not want to hear and yet it is a promise that brings with it untold blessings.

A promise which we love is the one which God made to Noah:

> *"Never again will I curse the ground because of man, even though every inclination of his heart is evil from childhood. And never again will I destroy all living creatures, as I have done. As long as the earth endures, seedtime and harvest, cold and heat, summer and winter, day and night will never cease."*
>
> *Genesis 8:20-22*

2

This is a marvellous promise because it is not dependant upon mankind fulfilling any conditions. It is one-sided if you like—all of God. I am so glad when we are given this kind of promise because if it were otherwise we would surely mess up and spoil everything.

In the next chapter God gives the sign of a rainbow to remind him of his everlasting covenant between him and all living creatures. Genesis 9:16

It is also a wonderful reminder to us that we are loved by God. Would God ever change his mind? No, of course not! Why not? Because he has stated that it is an everlasting covenant. Do we believe him? If we bring into question the promises of God then there is no certain hope, nor assurance of our salvation. Our future security is based on the words of Jesus:

> *"For God so loved the world that he gave his one and only Son, that whoever believes in him shall not perish but have eternal life."*
>
> *John 3:16*

> *"I am the way and the truth and the life. No one comes to the Father except through me."*
>
> *John 14:6*

These are familiar words to us but what if God changes his mind? This is of course not possible.

God spoke through Balaam an oracle to Balak:

> *"God is not a man, that he should lie, nor a son of man, that he should*

> *change his mind. Does he speak and then not act? Does he promise and not fulfil?"*
>
> Numbers 23:19

Towards of the end of his life, Joshua instructs his people:

> *"Now I am about to go the way of all the earth. You know with all your heart and soul that not one of all the good promises the Lord your God gave you has failed. Every promise has been fulfilled; not one has failed."*
>
> Joshua 23:14

The psalmist could say:

> *"I rejoice in your promise."*
>
> Psalm 119:162

We also revel in our Lord's wonderful promises to us and truthfully we can say that he has never failed us nor broken his word.

There is another promise of God—this time given to Moses. This is sometimes called the old covenant. This promise was made with the nation of Israel at Mount Sinai and is centred on the ten commandments:

> *"Now if you obey me fully and keep my covenant, then out of all the*

nations you will be my treasured possession."

Exodus 19:5

These commandments were itemised and we find them in Exodus 20 and later on when these commands had been explained and all the implications understood, Moses wrote them all out in a book (Exodus 24:4) and this was called the Book of the Covenant (v7). Many years later it was this book that was discovered during the time of King Josiah and the covenant was renewed. (2 Kings 23:2)

This promise was very different to that made to Noah because it contained the words, "if you obey."

That made it conditional upon the nation of Israel to obey these commands and if they didn't then God was not bound to fulfil his promise. Now we know that the Israelites failed to keep their side of the bargain and eventually turned their backs upon God and then paid a heavy price. Indeed they were forewarned just what would happen if they disobeyed God:

"If you do not follow all the words of this law . . . . so it will please him to ruin and destroy you. You will be uprooted from the land you are entering to possess. Then the Lord will scatter you among all the nations from one end of the earth to the other."

Deuteronomy 28:58-64

As we now know only too well this happened and the Jewish nation was first of all taken captive by the Babylonians and then finally routed by the Romans and scattered throughout the world. What a heavy price has been exacted upon the Jewish people over the centuries as they have been dispersed throughout the world yet it is amazing to note that they never lost their identity and after nearly 2,000 years they were re-established, as a nation, back in the land where it all started for them—in Israel. This was of course the fulfilment of another of God's promises:

> " . . . *the days are coming, declares the Lord, when people will no longer say, As surely as the Lord lives who brought the Israelites up out of Egypt, but they will say, As surely as the Lord lives, who brought the descendants of Israel up out of the north and out of all the countries where he had banished them. Then they will live in their own land."*
> *Jeremiah 23:7 & 8*

What a promise and what a fulfilment!

It is so important therefore to grasp that God does not make rash promises. As followers of Jesus Christ we delight in his words. Our ultimate salvation depends on his words being truthful and reliable. So can we depend upon God's promises? . . . Absolutely.

CHAPTER 2

What is so special about God's promises to Abraham?

Now that we have agreed that the promises of God can be relied on we move on to look at the promise that was made by God to Abram later to be called Abraham. It is called a Covenant because it is drawn up in a formal way. Many people have singled out this promise and have said in effect that the promise is no longer applicable. In other words God is not going to fulfil this promise.

Let us therefore go back to the beginning but more importantly go back to the word of God.

Terah was the father of Abram, and he decided to leave Ur of the Chaldeans with members of his family and journey to Haran, which is in the south of present day Turkey around sixty miles north of the River Euphrates. It is interesting to note that although scripture indicates that Terah made the decision to leave Ur, the Lord later says:

> *"I am the Lord, who brought you out of Ur of the Chaldeans to give you this land to take possession of it."*
> *Genesis 15:7*

How good it is to realise that the Lord himself can and does order the affairs of men.

Some years passed by and the family had settled into life in Haran. It is then that the Lord instructs Abram to leave Haran and journey to a land of the Lord's choosing. Abram was now 75 years old but the Lord gives Abram this wonderful promise:

> **"I will make you into a great nation and I will bless you, I will make your name great, and you will be a blessing. I will bless those who bless you, and whoever curses you I will curse; and all peoples on earth will be blessed through you."**
> **Genesis 12:2-3**

Many years later both Isaac and Jacob would find a bride from this area of Haran.

As Abram arrived in the land of Canaan he stopped at Shechem, present day Nablus, and again the Lord speaks to Abram:

> *"To your offspring I will give this land."*
> *Genesis 12:7*

Time passes, there is a famine and Abraham goes to Egypt to live there for a while and we read that when he returns to the southern part of the land of Israel, the Negev, he is now very wealthy with livestock, silver and gold. It is evident that he moves around the land with his livestock in order to find grazing and comes at last to a place near Bethel, a few miles north of Jerusalem. From this elevated place it is possible to see the Mediterranean Sea in the west and the Jordan Valley and the Dead Sea in the east. It is from here that Abraham and his nephew, Lot, part company, with Lot opting to take his herds down to the plains of Sodom at the southern end of the Dead Sea.

It is then that the Lord speaks again to Abram. How wonderful it is when we hear the Lord speaking to us. This is what he said on this occasion:

> *"Lift up your eyes from where you are and look north and south, east and west. All the land that you see I will give to you and your offspring for ever. I will make your offspring like the dust of the earth, so that if anyone could count the dust, then your offspring could be counted. Go walk through the length and breadth of the land, for I am giving it to you."*
> *Genesis 13:15-17*

This is the third time now God has made promises to Abram.

He promised that a great nation would descend from Abram, and other nations, depending upon their attitude to his descendants, would receive God's blessing or cursing. Abram was also promised all the land that he could see though at this stage the borders had not been defined.

The Lord speaks to Abram again:

> *"Do not be afraid, Abram. I am your shield, your very great reward."*
>
> *Genesis 15:1*

It is interesting to note the Hebrew word m*agen* for shield is mentioned for the first time here in the word of God. The Star of David which features on the Israeli flag is made up of two triangular shields.

Abram however has two problems. The first was concerning this great nation of which he was to be the father of. He has no children and as far as he was concerned Eliezer, his servant, stood to inherit all he had. The Lord quickly tells him that he will indeed produce a son and brought Abram outside under the night sky:

> *"Look up at the heavens and count the stars—if indeed you can count them. So shall your seed be."*
>
> *Genesis 15:5*

Previously Abram's seed had been likened to the dust of the earth now it is the stars in the heaven. Which has the greatest number? Apparently there are more stars, incredible as it may seem. And to answer the Lord's statement, no we cannot count them even with our high powered telescopes and far flung satellites.

After the Lord has reiterated that Abram was to take possession of this land Abram raises his second problem:

> *"O Sovereign Lord, how can I know*
> *that I shall gain possession of it?"*
> *Genesis 15:8*

What followed was without precedent and gives us an insight as to the importance of the promise that the Lord had already made. The Lord could have told Abram just to trust Him and that would have been sufficient. Our Lord chose, however, to make a covenant in a special way and this was to be by sacrifice. The way God made this covenant with Abram is described in detail (v12) it was to be by sacrifice and we are told a little more about the method in Jeremiah 34:18. First a heifer, goat and ram were slain and cut into two pieces and placed opposite their respective halves. A dove and pigeon were also placed in formation, leaving a pathway between. Then the parties making the covenant walked between the pieces. The way it happened, as I understand it, was that the two men stood back to back and walked away from each other in a figure of eight, in between the pieces of the torn sacrifice, and then came together facing each other. They in effect pledged their lives to its fulfilment and called down upon themselves the fate of the slain animals in case of unfaithfulness. It was to be different however when God cut his covenant with Abram because God put Abram into a "deep sleep" thus preventing him from passing through the slain sacrifice.

It had been an amazing 24 hours for Abram. On the previous night God had showed him the stars and during the day he had been preparing the sacrifice and making sure the birds did not eat it. Now the sun was setting again and as he sleeps God reveals a little of how Abram's descendants would fare. It was not all good news. But then through the pattern of the sacrifice moves a smoking brazier with flames shooting out. Instead of two parties making the covenant, God is confirming it on his own. We are not told but I assume that the flames devoured up the sacrifice. The narrative finishes this passage as follows:

> *"On that day the Lord made a covenant with Abram and said, To your descendants I give this land, from the river of Egypt to the great river, the Euphrates . . . ."*
>
> *Genesis 15:18*

Then follows a list of the people who would be displaced.

It is assumed the river of Egypt is not the Nile but Wadi el Arish as mentioned in Numbers 34:5.

This incident is referred to many years later:

> *"When God made His promise to Abraham, since there was no one*

> *greater for Him to swear by, He swore by Himself."*
>
> *Hebrews 6:13*

The writer to the Hebrews is emphasising just how much we can rely on God's promises. He selects this promise as an example and says:

> *"Because God wanted to make the unchanging nature of his purpose very clear to the heirs of what was promised, he confirmed it with an oath. God did this so that, by two unchangeable things in which it is impossible for God to lie, we who have fled to take hold of the hope offered to us may be greatly encouraged. We have this hope as an anchor for the soul, firm and secure . . . ."*
>
> *Hebrews 6:17-19*

In other words if we are looking for assurance for our salvation we need look no further than Gods promise to Abram. God's promises can be relied upon.

Before we leave this event there are one or two other points we should note.

What was Abram's part in this covenant? What did he have to do? Nothing! Not a thing.

This was the Almighty God swearing by himself that he was going to fulfill this promise.

So what did Abram agree to? Nothing! Not a thing. After all he was asleep!

It is what is known as an unconditional promise. No conditions were attached.

Time passes and Abram is now 99 years old. 13 years earlier Abram and his wife Sarai thought that the only way that they were going to have a child was if Abram slept with the maidservant, Hagar. She gave birth to a son and he was named Ishmael by the angel of the Lord.

Ah, how impatient we are with the Lord sometimes.

Now the Lord speaks with Abram again and tells him that his name is being changed to Abraham, which means father of many:

> " . . . for I have made you a father of many nations. I will make you very fruitful. I will make nations of you, and kings will come from you. I will establish my covenant as an everlasting covenant between me and you and your descendants after you for the generations to come, to be your God and the God of your descendants after you. The whole land of Canaan where you are now an alien, I will as an everlasting possession to you and your descendants after you, and I will be their God."
>
> *Genesis 17:5-8*

Twice over here the Lord God uses the word everlasting. An everlasting covenant and an everlasting possession.

This is an amazing promise—no conditions and it just keeps going.

Just as God keeps his promises so also he means what he says. We have already looked at the words which are found in the letter to the Hebrews which said that because God keeps his promise we have a hope which is just like an anchor for the soul, firm and secure.

Now if we start chipping away at this promise then we have no right to claim that the life we have been given as recorded in John 3:16 is everlasting. We claim that because of what the Lord has promised to us, we have eternal life. John also writes as follows:

> *"I write these things to you who believe in the name of the Son of God so that you may know that you have eternal life."*
>
> *1 John 5:13*

We are in no doubt—we have eternal life—even so can the promise to Abraham be relied upon.

Just as the rainbow was set in the sky as a sign of the covenant with Noah so God instituted the practice of circumcision as the sign for this covenant. Genesis 17:11

Just as the Lord God had promised, Abraham did become the father of a great multitude and many nations claim him as their father. But who would take possession of the promises which God had made to Abraham? We are left in no doubt. Sarai's name is changed to Sarah:

> *"I will bless her and will surely give you a son by her. I will bless her so that she will be the mother of nations, kings of peoples will come from her."*
> *Genesis 17:16*

Abraham then questions God about Ishmael:

> *"If only Ishmael might live under your blessing!"*
> *v 18*

The answer is so important that we will quote it in full:

> *"Then God said, 'Yes, but your wife Sarah will bear you a son, and you will call him Isaac. I will establish my covenant with him as an everlasting covenant for his descendants after him. And as for Ishmael, I have heard you: I will surely bless him; I will make him fruitful and will increase his numbers. He will be the father of twelve rulers, and I will make him into a great nation. But my covenant I will establish Isaac, whom Sarah will bear to you by this time next year.'"*
> *vs 19-21*

So there we have it the promises of God will be continued down through the line of Isaac.

Time passes and the miraculous birth of Isaac occurs, and then as the years slip by God requests that Abraham takes his son Isaac and sacrifice him on a mount which would later be called Moriah. After the angel of the Lord intervenes, another message is received from on high:

> *"I swear by myself, declares the Lord, that because you have done this and have not withheld your son, your only son, I will surely bless you and make your descendants as numerous as the stars in the sky and as the sand on the seashore. Your descendants will take possession of the cities of their enemies, and through your offspring all nations on the earth will be blessed, because you have obeyed me."*
>
> *Genesis 22:17-18*

It all seems very familiar. Abraham already knew all this! We have already pondered over these details, yet here it as again. How comforting it is when we receive confirmation of God's will for our lives.

Years pass by. Abraham and Sarah die and we follow the progress of Isaac. Would God reveal himself to Isaac as he did to his father? Indeed he would. A famine occurs and Isaac debates whether he should go to Egypt. The Lord God speaks:

> *"Stay in this land for a while, and I will be with you and will bless you. For to you and your descendants I will give all these lands and will confirm the oath I swore to your father Abraham. I will make your descendants as numerous as the stars in the sky and will give them all these lands, and through your offspring all nations on earth will be blessed, because Abraham obeyed me . . ."*
>
> *Genesis 26:3-5*

How wonderful to have such a promise renewed by the Lord himself.

Let us just follow the line of this promise a little further. Isaac has twin boys with his wife Rebekah, Jacob and Esau. The Lord indicates that from these two boys will spring two nations. It is important therefore to be sure which would inherit the vital promises of God.

Now we know that Jacob tricked his brother out of his birthright and received the blessing from his father Isaac, but what about the promises which the Lord had made to Abraham and then to Isaac?

Jacob is on his way to Haran to find a bride. He stops at Luz, which will soon become Bethel, and with a stony pillow he dreams and sees in his dream a ladder reaching into heaven itself. Angels of God were going up and down and above it all stood the Lord himself. He speaks:

"I am the Lord, the God of your father Abraham and the God of Isaac. I will give you and your descendants the land on which you are lying. Your descendants will be like the dust of the earth and you will spread out to the west and to the east, to the north and to the south. All peoples on earth will be blessed through you and your offspring. I am with you and will watch over you wherever you go, and I will bring you back to this land. I will not leave you until I have done what I have promised to you."

Genesis 28:13-15

Twenty years roll by and Jacob is found back in the same place, Bethel, this time with wives, children and livestock. Again the Lord God appears to him:

"Your name is Jacob but you will no longer be called Jacob; your name will be Israel. I am God Almighty, be fruitful and increase in number. A nation and a community of nations will come from you, and kings will come from your body. The land I gave to Abraham and Isaac I also give to you, and I will give this land to your descendants after you."

Genesis 35:10-12

We are left in no doubt therefore as to whom the promises are bound for. Jacob now called Israel has twelve children henceforth to be known as the children of Israel and the rest as they say is history.

One of the reasons why the Lord God brought the children of Israel out of Egypt was because of his promise to Abraham. Listen to what he says to Moses:

> *"I am the Lord. I appeared to Abraham, to Isaac and to Jacob as God Almighty, but by my name the Lord I did not make myself known to them. I also established my covenant with them to give them the land of Canaan, where they lived as aliens. Moreover, I have heard the groaning of the Israelites, whom the Egyptians are enslaving, and I have remembered my covenant."*
>
> *Exodus 6:2-5*

After Joshua led the Children of Israel back to the Promised Land we read:

> *"So the Lord gave Israel all the land he had sworn to give their forefathers, and they took possession of it and settled there."*
>
> *Joshua 21:43*

Nehemiah, in his prayer of confession, following the peoples return from exile in Babylon mentions

the covenant which God made to Abraham.
Nehemiah 9:8

Many years later Peter and John speak to the
assembled Jewish gathering in the temple precincts
after healing a lame man:

> *"And you are heirs of the prophets*
> *and of the covenant God made with*
> *your fathers. He said to Abraham.*
> *Through your offspring all peoples on*
> *earth will be blessed."*
>
> *Acts 3:25*

Why has the Lord gone to such lengths to repeat
his promises on so many different occasions?

Once would have been sufficient! You may
have thought that but we humans are fickle folk
and often think that we have better ideas than God
himself.

One last verse on this subject:

> *"He remembers his covenant for*
> *ever, the word he commanded for a*
> *thousand generations, the covenant*
> *he made with Abraham, the oath*
> *he swore to Isaac. He confirmed it*
> *to Jacob as a decree, to Israel as an*
> *everlasting covenant. To you I will*
> *give the land of Canaan as the portion*
> *you will inherit."*
>
> *Psalm 105:8-11*

We now see that this promise which has now been repeated to three different people is unconditional, irrevocable and everlasting.

With such a weight of documentation for these promises and much more that we have not looked at, how is it that so many even within the church are prepared to deny their relevance for today?

CHAPTER 3

Why Israel?

I awoke with a jolt. I had overslept and it was unforgivable for a tour leader to be late. Rushing round the room, I collected all the bits and pieces I needed for the day ahead, threw them into my bag and ran outside. It was eerily quiet. We were staying on a kibbutz on the western side of Lake Galilee which was handily placed for us to visit many of the sites which Jesus had frequented. One or two of the kibbutz staff were making their way to the kitchen. Something was not right! I looked at my watch again—it was only 6am—I had misread the time and rather than being late I was an hour early! Feeling such a fool I decided that rather than going back into my room I would wander down to the lakeside and watch the sunrise. The morning was still, very still. The sky was cloudless. It was going to be a very warm day. The water level of the lake was low and in order to allow the boats to come alongside the pier, temporary extensions had been added. I decided that I would walk to the end and stood over the water looking across the lake to the Golan Heights over which the sun would shortly rise. This was good. I began to feel that the Lord had yanked me out of bed so that He could spend some time with me. I acknowledged to myself that I didn't spend enough quality time with the Lord.

What happened next will remain indelibly in my memory for all time. The sun began to rise and like a floodlight shone its light and warmth onto my face. At the same time two kingfishers appeared and hovered over the waters one on either side of me. From nowhere a flock of swallows suddenly flew past but then they divided into two groups again one on either side of me and started to fly towards each other like soldiers inter-marching only this was at break neck speed. I stood transfixed as the birds performed their routine. Transfixed possibly because if I moved I reckoned that I might be struck as the swallows were whistling past my nose with little space to spare. It seemed as though the fly past went on for a long time but it could only have been for a minute or so. At a hidden signal manoeuvres stopped and I was left looking across the lake at the sun which by now had completely emerged from behind the hills opposite. I turned and was amazed to see that the swallows were all standing in a long line on the handrail of the pier just beside me. In unison they all bowed and flew off—the show was finished the swallows and kingfishers were gone and I was left . . . in tears.

"What was all that about?" I said to myself. Was the Lord trying to tell me something? Then a little voice inside said, "No. I did it just for you, because I love you!"

But why me?

The question is often asked as to why God chose Israel to set his affections on in such a remarkable way. These folk must have been very special people that God should love them so much? In fact this was not the case:

> *"The Lord did not set his affection on you and choose you because you were more numerous than other peoples, for you were the fewest of all peoples. But it was because the Lord loved you and kept the oath he swore to your forefathers that he brought you out with a mighty hand and redeemed you from the hand of slavery, from the power of Pharaoh king of Egypt. Know therefore that the Lord your God, he is the faithful God, keeping the covenant of love to a thousand generations . . . ."*
>
> *Deuteronomy 7:7-9*

The scriptures tell it as it was, warts and all! The Israelites were sometimes described as stiff necked, stubborn, obstinate, disobedient and treacherous toward God, but even with all these failings stacked against them, God remains faithful to his promises. Listen to what the Lord God says again:

> *"I will remember my covenant with Jacob, and my covenant with Isaac and my covenant with Abraham, and I will remember the land. For the land will be deserted by them and will enjoy its Sabbaths while it lies desolate without them. They will pay for their sins because they rejected my laws and abhorred my decrees. Yet in spite of this, when they are in the land of their enemies, I will not reject them or abhor them so as to destroy them completely, breaking my covenant with them. I am the Lord their God. But for their sake I will remember the covenant with their ancestors whom I brought out of Egypt in the sight of the nations to be their God. I am the Lord."*
>
> *Leviticus 26:42 & 45*

God, in his sovereign will determined that it would be from this line of Israel that the Messiah would be born, our Saviour. We cannot say, "Why?" Can the clay say to the potter, "Why me?"

It is often said that some Jewish people today question why God chose them and wish it was not so.

But ponder awhile and muse upon God's dealings with you and me. Why did God set his affections upon us?

> *"God demonstrates his own love for*
> *us in this: While we were yet sinners,*
> *Christ died for us."*
> *Romans 5:8*

If God dealt with us according to what we deserve then there would be no hope for any of us.

Before we get too hung up about God favouring Israel above all other nations let us go back to the original promise which contains the words,

"All peoples of the earth will be blessed through you and your offspring."

Because of God blessing Abraham and Isaac and Israel, we too are blessed.

Note also that Abraham was born two years after Noah died. The earth's population was relatively small and nations had not been formed. It was to be a future nation that God would bless, a nation into which our Lord was born. After we have finished all of our protestations the fact remains, the nation of Israel was and is chosen of God:

> *"For you are a people holy to the*
> *Lord your God. The Lord your God*
> *has chosen you out of all the peoples*
> *on the face of the earth to be his*
> *people, his treasured possession."*
> *Deuteronomy 7:6*

Well Israel may have been chosen, some say, but they blew it! They crucified the Christ and that was their undoing. Now it's the turn of the Church.

Let us see what the scriptures say about this. We do of course believe that the scriptures are the inspired Word of God. Don't we?

> *"This is what the Lord says, he who appoints the sun to shine by day, who decrees the moon and stars to shine by night, who stirs up the sea so that its waves roar—the Lord almighty is his name: only if these decrees vanish from my sight declares the Lord will the descendants of Israel ever cease to be a nation before me. Only if the heavens above can be measured and the foundations of the earth below be searched out will I reject all the descendants of Israel because of all they have done, declares the Lord."*
>
> *Jeremiah 31:35-37*

As long as the sun, moon, earth and sea are there; there will be a distinct people of Israel—that is God's promise! We have seen and are still seeing the miracle of Israel unfold before our eyes. Great was their blessing, great too their responsibility. Truly they were scattered as a nation to the four corners of the earth. But look what is happening:

> *"Hear the word of the Lord, O nations; proclaim it in distant coastlands. He who scattered Israel*

will gather them and will watch over his flock like a shepherd."

Jeremiah 31:10

The Jewish people are flocking back to their homeland in Israel. After 2000 years they have not lost their identity and with a revived Hebrew language they rebuild just as was prophesied:

"Do not be afraid, for I am with you; I will bring your children from the east and gather you from the west, I will say to the north, 'Give them up!' and to the south, 'Do not hold them back.' Bring my sons from afar and my daughters from the ends of the earth . . ."

Isaiah 43:5-6

Just in case there was any doubt that this prophecy was only in respect of the Babylonian captivity, notice that the return is from all directions.

This theme is often spoken about in scripture:

"This is what the Lord Almighty says: 'I will save my people from the countries of the east and the west. I will bring them back to live in Jerusalem; they will be my people, and I will be faithful and righteous to them as their God.'"

Zechariah 8:7-8

What we are seeing in our day the Bible commentators of your grandparents days could only dream about. We are witnessing something that is of more significance than the exodus from Egypt. Why do I say that? Because the scriptures tell us:

> *"However, the days are coming, declares the Lord, when men will no longer say, 'As surely as the Lord lives who brought the Israelites up out of Egypt,' but they will say, 'As surely as the Lord lives, who brought the Israelites up out of the land of the north and out of all the countries where he had banished them.' For I will restore them to the land I gave to their forefathers."*
>
> *Jeremiah 16:14-15*

But what if Israel broke the covenant? Well first of all there were no conditions to break. But what if the people turned away from God and God had to punish them?

> *"Though I completely destroy all the nations among which I scatter you, I will not completely destroy you. I will discipline you but only with justice; I will not let you go entirely unpunished."*
>
> *Jeremiah 30:11*

Now you would think that Christians worldwide would be rejoicing as they see the literal fulfilment of scripture coming to pass. Not so.

Why is it that many denominations of the Christian Church have pulled away from supporting Israel? Why is that respectable charities, who claim to have a Christian ethos, no longer support Israel?

Why is it that certain Arab countries seek the entire elimination of Israel?

Why is it that United Nations raises more Resolutions against Israel than any other country?

Why is it that the Human Rights Council has adopted more resolutions condemning Israel than it has all other states combined whilst often totally ignoring world atrocities?

Whilst many, if not all, of these bodies would vehemently reject my proposal, I believe that they are bowing to a satanic agenda.

Consider the time before the advent of Jesus Christ. Satan tried his utmost to corrupt the line from which the Messiah would be born and even to tempt the Lord himself into committing sin and thus thwart God's plan of salvation.

From the very beginning we read that Satan tempted Adam and Eve to rebel against God and from that time Satan sought to interrupt the Godly line. Cain slew his brother:

> *"Do not be like Cain, who belonged to the evil one and murdered his brother."*
>
> 1 John 3:12

Prior to the flood Satan tried to corrupt the entire human race by supernatural means. The sons of God intermarried with humankind. Sons of God were associated with Satan (Job 1:6 & Job 2:1) and the result of this union was:

> *"The Lord saw how great man's wickedness on earth had become, and that every inclination of the thoughts of his heart was only evil all the time."*
>
> *Genesis 7:5*

So devastating was the result of this satanic attack that God caused a flood to wipe out mankind apart from Noah and his immediate family. As for the offending angels:

> *"The angels who did not keep their positions of authority but abandoned their own home—these he has kept in darkness, bound with everlasting chains for judgement on the Great Day."*
>
> *Jude:6*

We can no doubt think of many more attacks such as that of Haman:

> *"to destroy, kill and annihilate all the Jews—young and old, woman and little children on a single day."*
>
> *Esther 3:13*

It did not stop there:

> *"Come, they say, let us destroy them as a nation, that the name of Israel be remembered no more.*
>
> *"Psalm 83:4*

> *"The word of the Lord came to Jeremiah: Have you not noticed that these people are saying, 'The Lord has rejected the two kingdoms he chose?' So they despise my people and no longer regard them as a nation."*
>
> *Jeremiah 33:23-24*

Herod plots to kill the newly born Christ child unsuccessfully and finally Satan himself enters into Judas. Luke 22:3

Now consider further. Satan failed in his attempt to corrupt our Lord. He now knows that Jesus has conquered the power of death and the consequence of sin. So how can he further thwart the purposes of God? Does he know the scriptures? Oh yes. He was able to misquote them as he tempted Jesus Christ during his time in the wilderness. He therefore also knows where the Lord will return to earth:

> *"On that day his feet will stand on the Mount of Olives, east of Jerusalem . . ."*
>
> *Zechariah 14:4*

The Lord will come to rescue the Jewish from their enemies and from the severe persecution which they will be suffering at time. If there are, however, no Jewish people in the land, then the Lord will not come. Such is Satan's thinking.

He will use all means at his disposal to rid the world of Jewish people whether by war or delegitimisation.

Like every other country, Israel makes mistakes. Remember Israel is largely a secular country. The majority do not follow the Lord God and few read the scriptures. One day this will change and the scales will fall from their eyes but it will be the Lord's timing.

It behoves us therefore to examine our hearts and the motives behind the actions we take and the bodies that we support.

CHAPTER 4

What has this old covenant got to do with me as we have a new one?

T he apostle Paul was a Jew. He never concealed this fact. On entering a new town on his missionary journeys he first of all went to the synagogue. He had a deep longing for his own people that they would recognise Christ as their Messiah. Listen to what he says:

> "I have great sorrow and unceasing anguish in my heart. For I could wish that I myself were cursed and cut off from Christ for the sake of my brothers, those of my own race, the people of Israel. Theirs is the adoption as sons; theirs the divine glory, the covenants, the receiving of the law, the temple worship and the

> *promises. Theirs are the patriarchs,*
> *and from them is traced the human*
> *ancestry of Christ, who is God over*
> *all, for ever praised! Amen."*
> *Romans 9:3-5*

We can almost feel his grief as he recounts all the blessings which have been bestowed upon his countrymen. Did you notice what is included in this wonderful list? The covenants!

But surely we know this. We have been thinking about some of these covenants and yes we agree that they were given to the ancient Israelite peoples.

The new covenant, however, was given to the Gentiles. Right? Wrong!

Listen again to the words of scripture:

> *"The time is coming, declares the*
> *Lord, when I will make a new*
> *covenant with the house of Israel and*
> *with the house of Judah . . ."*
> *Jeremiah 31:31*

This passage of scripture is repeated in Hebrews 8:8-12 and is the longest Old Testament quotation to be found in the New Testament.

What does this mean? It means that Israel has everything including all the promises. The new covenant was for the law to be written in minds and hearts rather than on tablets of stone. It was a new way whereby the temporary sacrifices would come to an end with the sacrifice of Christ and instead of the burden of sin being constantly carried around; God said that

> *"I will remember their sins no more."*
> *Hebrews 8 :12*

So what about Gentiles surely they can participate in God's great salvation? Indeed they can.

Listen again to what Paul says about our inheritance in Christ:

> "You are all sons of God through faith in Christ, for all of you who were baptised into Christ have clothed yourselves with Christ. There is neither Jew nor Greek, slave nor free, male nor female, for you are all one in Christ Jesus. **If you belong to Christ, then you are Abraham's seed, and heirs according to the promise.**"

Now we have already established that God's promises to Abraham were everlasting and were made exclusively to him and his descendents through Isaac and Jacob. Now the blessings which were given to Abraham can also apply to Gentile believers because they belong to Christ. How marvellous!

Why then would any thinking Christian want to get rid of the promises and to the attached blessings which God made to Abraham? Why surrender your inheritance?

CHAPTER 5

The Palestine problem

It had been snowing overnight and the palm trees looked surreal with a coating of snow. We had been staying for a few days in Bethlehem which, of course, is situated in the West Bank. I had a few free hours so decided to have a wander. Along the Main Street the young folk seemed bemused to see the snow and true to form it was not long before I had to dodge a hail of snowballs which came from a group of young lads. The sun was getting hotter and it would not be long before all trace of the snow would be gone. In the distance I could see a local bakery and soon I could smell the wonderful aroma of freshly baked bread. Two young men approached me who already were feasting on the new bread. They stopped me and offered to share their bread with me. I accepted their kind invitation and they proceeded to break off a piece of bread. It tasted good! I thought, how appropriate that in Bethlehem—Beit Lechem meaning House of Bread,

I should be offered such a gift. I continued my walk down into the valley below the town. I wandered through ancient terraces which had been created many centuries ago. Some were in a poor state of repair. Others were tended with olive trees growing in abundance. I thought just what had taken place right here over the years. A broken water cistern was there but was now only a shelter for sheep but who created it and how long ago? I nearly stepped on a tortoise and stopped to watch it trudge away. I had never given thought to where they came from. A snake slithered away as my feet broke a twig—yes this was Judea. Just then I came across a building which was broken down, but what had it been? It was a watch tower! Just what action had this tower seen? How many times had Bethlehem come under attack even back to the time of David? After all it was called the City of David. Ah, and even to this day there is not peace. Surely everyone wants peace.

Not so many years ago everyone was quite comfortable with the name Palestine. It symbolised the Holy Land. It was the name we had grown up with. On perusing Bible commentaries from the last century it becomes evident that authors even equated Palestine with the place where Jesus walked. Over recent years however the picture has changed and has taken on more political significance. It is important therefore to examine the history of Palestine as this will determine our attitude towards Israel.

Jesus did not walk in Palestine. His ministry was conducted throughout Judea, Samaria and mostly Galilee. Palestine did not exist then. It all came about in this way. Following the final Jewish revolt against the Romans during AD132-135, Emperor Hadrian ransacked Jerusalem with the bulk of the Jewish population being captured, killed, or escaping to foreign lands. He changed the name of Jerusalem to Aeolia Capitolina and as a final insult to the Jews he changed the name of the country to Provincia Syria Palaestina after their long time enemies, Syria and the Philistines. The Philistines had gone from the scene many years before being finally routed by Alexander the Great and do not get a mention in the New Testament. Other than the departure of Jewish population there was no change in the ethnic make up of the nation—it was simply a name change. As years went by the name was shortened and anglicised to Palestine.

History records the many times that Israel was invaded from that time but latterly it became part of the Ottoman Empire from 1517 to 1917. In the early years of this period much building work was done such as the present walls of the old city of Jerusalem but as the years rolled by it fell into disrepair and the Ottomans became something of an absentee landlord.

The land became desolate. In the 1840's, David Roberts travelled extensively in the Middle East and drew and sketched many pictures of the Holy Land which give a good idea of how forsaken it was.

Mark Twain travelled from Damascus through Israel on horseback in 1869. In his book, The Innocents Abroad, he describes what he saw:

Of the Hula Valley—"There is not a solitary village throughout its whole extent—not for thirty miles in either direction. There are two or three small clusters of Bedouin tents, but not a single permanent habitation. One may ride ten miles hereabouts, and not see ten human beings."

From Galilee to Mount Tabor, "We never saw a human being on the whole route."

Of Jerusalem: "So small. Why it was no larger than an American village of four thousand inhabitants . . ."

Looking back on his visit through the land, Mark Twain said: "Of all the lands there for dismal scenery, I think Palestine must be the prince."

He continued: "Palestine sits in sackcloth and ashes. Over it broods the spell of a curse that has withered its fields and fettered its energies."

He acknowledged that there were beautiful spots but these were "set at wide intervals in a waste of limitless desolation."

How awful that a land with such resources and promise could be described in such a way. Yet even this was prophesied long ago:

> *"Therefore because of you, Zion will be ploughed like a field, Jerusalem will become a heap of rubble, the temple hill a mound overgrown with thickets."*
>
> *Micah 3:12*

The land was desolate until the early 1880's when Zionist pioneers began to trickle back into the land. The early pioneers bought land and quickly began to drain & cultivate the land. They needed labour for this and Arabs from the surrounding countries soon learned that work was to be had and moved in with their families and settled alongside the pioneers. The Arabs soon outnumbered the early settlers.

The Ottoman Empire ended in 1917 when Turkey sided with Germany in World War 1. On 2 November of the same year, UK's Foreign Secretary, Arthur James Balfour wrote a letter to Baron Rothschild, a leader of the British Jewish Community:

"His Majesty's government view with favour the establishment in Palestine of a national home for the Jewish people, and will use their best endeavours to facilitate the achievement of this object, it being clearly understood that nothing shall be done which may prejudice the civil and religious rights of existing non-Jewish communities in Palestine, or the rights and political status enjoyed by Jews in any other country."

This letter became known as the Balfour Declaration and set in motion the recognition of a state of Israel once again.

In the years following other Arab countries, which had previously been part of the Ottoman Empire, were formed and borders determined. In all 22 Arab countries were established as they are today having a total area of 5,148,048 square miles. Israel was allotted 10,840 square miles with its length being 290 miles and width 85miles

So it came to be that Israel was surrounded by countries that were hostile to its formation as an independent state. Indeed the Arab/Islamic areas cover vast areas of the Middle East and beyond, so when the Declaration of Independence was signed in 1948 it came as no surprise that The War of Independence ensued the following day.

The trickle of Jewish immigrants increased during the British Mandate and following the dreadful events of World War 2 the trickle turned into a river.

When was it then that the Arabs who were residing in Israel decided to call themselves Palestinians?

Yasser Arafat quoted the following in 1968 after being defeated by Israel in the 6 day war:

> "We plan to eliminate the state of Israel and establish a purely Palestinian state. We will make life unbearable for Jews by

> psychological warfare and population explosion . . . We Palestinians will take over everything including all of Jerusalem."
>
> He went on to officially declare Palestine a state in Algiers on 15 November 1988.

As Christians we believe that all mankind is loved by God and all can receive salvation through our Lord Jesus Christ. We therefore bear no animosity towards our Arab brethren, however, with all the vast lands which the Arabs own it would seem unreasonable to snatch away the little tract of land which is known as Israel. There have always been aliens living within Israel's borders even in Biblical times. Provision was always made for them within the law.

At present there are over one and a half million Arabs living within the internationally agreed borders of Israel representing around 20% of the population. Many of these Arabs live in recognised Arab towns and communities and most have taken out Israeli citizenship. Conversely half a million Jews live in so called settlements in the West Bank although many of these dwell in suburbs of Jerusalem which has spread out over the years.

Many heads of State around the world call for a two state solution. This will be very difficult to achieve given the underlying aim of the Arab world to eliminate the state of Israel, it will be a case of just giving more land away for nothing in return and making the remaining land which Israel will have indefensible. Resolutions may be passed in the United Nations in favour of a Palestinian state but without the Arab nations recognising the existence of Israel as a Jewish state, a long term peace will never be achieved.

It may be that we will have to wait for the anti-christ to arrive on the scene, who will establish a false peace:

> *"He will confirm a covenant with many for one seven. In the middle of the seven he will put an end to sacrifice and offering. And on a wing of the temple he will set up an abomination that causes desolation, until the end that is decreed is poured out on him."*
>
> Daniel 9:27

So it seems as though the world is against Israel and we have campaigns to divest from Israel. Churches and charities, companies and governments boycott goods which are produced not only in the West Bank but also from Israel itself. Terms such as occupied territories and apartheid are bandied about when nothing could be further from the truth. Israel is the only true democracy in the Middle East even to having Arab members of the Knesset. The reason for erecting a security fence/wall is soon forgotten by the world but Israel still bears the scars of suicide bombing and terrorist attacks.

There is a far more sinister reason for these actions against Israel and eternity will reveal how Satan used God's redeemed people to attempt to thwart God's purposes.

Here is the issue. On the one hand we have the promises of God granting all the land of Israel to the descendents of Abraham through the line of Isaac and Jacob. On the other we have part of these lands being occupied by the Arabs and wanting more even to half of Jerusalem. The biblical history of the various towns in the West Bank as belonging to Israel is undoubted.

Jericho was taken by Joshua.

Shechem (now Nablus) was the place first visited by Abraham; Joshua addressed the tribes of Israel here; Abimelech and Rehoboam were elected king here by the inhabitants.

Hebron was given to Caleb by Joshua. David was king here for seven years.

Ramah now Ramallah is the birth place of Samuel near to Bethel where God confirmed his promises to Jacob.

Bethlehem—we all know about Bethlehem.

We could go on but it is not necessary for the whole of Israel is well documented as being owned and dwelt in by the Israelite peoples in Biblical times. In fact the documentary evidence is overwhelming. Take a look at Nehemiah chapter 7—we see there that families are listed by name who, both left their towns to go into the Babylonian exile and then returned to the same towns together with the numbers of people who were involved. How amazing is that!

After various wars waged upon Israel by their neighbours, some land has been regained by Israel. Is it to be returned? These are the issues which successive world leaders have sought to solve but if they do not accept that the Promises of God are valid they are not likely to arrive at the correct solution.

Our sovereign God will prevail despite what the world may think:

> *"There is a river whose streams make glad the city of God, the holy place where the Most High dwells. God is within her, she will not fall; God will help her at break of day. Nations are in uproar, kingdoms fall; he lifts his voice, the earth melts."*
>
> *Psalm 46:4-6*

CHAPTER 6

What is Israel's future?

P aul describes what has happened to Israel as a mystery. The mystery however is explained to us:

> *"I do not want you to be ignorant of this mystery, brothers, so that you may not be conceited. Israel has experienced a hardening in part until the full number of the Gentiles has come in."*
> *Romans 11:25-26*

Perhaps it is akin to the hardening of Pharaoh's heart when he would not let the Children of Israel go from Egypt. Thus because of the rejection of Jesus as their Messiah by the Jewish people the gospel has been given to the Gentiles. Please note that this verse says **until** the full number of the Gentiles has come in. One day, which is drawing ever nearer, the last Gentile will be saved and God will again turn his attention towards the Jewish folk.

Paul goes on to say:

> *"As far as the gospel is concerned, they are enemies on your account; but as far as election is concerned, they are loved on account of the patriarchs, for God's gifts and his call are irrevocable."*
>
> Romans 11:28-29

Many people today assume that God has turned away from the Jewish people as they have had their last chance. Paul anticipates this meets it head on:

> *"I ask then: Did God reject his people? By no means!"*
>
> Romans 11:1

> *"Again I ask: Did they stumble so as to fall beyond recovery? Not at all! Rather, because of their transgression salvation has come to the Gentiles to make Israel envious."*
>
> Romans 11:11

In order to explain the position a little more we have the picture of an olive tree. The olive tree with roots represents the Jewish people:

> *"If some of the branches have been broken off, and you, though a wild olive shoot, have been grafted in among the others and now share*

*in the nourishing sap from the
olive root, do not boast over those
branches. If you do, consider this:
you do not support the root, but the
root supports you."*

Romans 11:17-18

So will the Jews be brought back into fellowship
with the Lord? Yes indeed they will! Listen again:

*"If they do not persist in unbelief,
they will be grafted in, for God is
able to graft them in again. After all,
if you were cut out of an olive tree
that is wild by nature, and contrary to
nature were grafted into a cultivated
olive tree, how much more readily
will these, the natural branches, be
grafted into their own olive tree!"*

Romans 11:23-24

Not far from Jaffa Gate in the old city of
Jerusalem lies Christ Church. It is a beautiful if
fairly plain looking church and I doubt that many
groups visiting the Holy Land will include it on their
itinerary. The first time I visited the church I stood
gazing for a time at two stained glass windows at
the front of the church. The magnificent windows
depict olive trees with branches that have been cut
off and from these branches others had been grafted
on and they rise in the form of a cross. Underneath
each window is Hebrew script which was difficult to
understand even for those who knew the language.

After making enquiries the translation under one was "for God's gift and his call are irrevocable." Under the other window, "they too may now receive mercy as a result of God's mercy to you."

How wonderful, that one day we Gentile and Jewish believers will together join hands and sing the praises of our dear Saviour.

As far as the land of Israel is concerned, we are already seeing the fulfilment of prophecy:

> *"The desolate land will be cultivated instead of lying desolate in the sight of all who pass through it. They will say, 'This land that was laid waste has become like the Garden of Eden;' the cities that were lying in ruins, desolate and destroyed, are now fortified and inhabited. Then the nations around you that remain will know that I the Lord have rebuilt what was destroyed and have replanted what was desolate. I the Lord have spoken, and I will do it."*
>
> *Ezekiel 36:34-36*

> *"The Lord will surely comfort Zion and will look with compassion on all her ruins; he will make her deserts like Eden, her wastelands like the garden of the Lord. Joy and gladness will be found in her, thanksgiving and the sounds of singing."*
>
> *Isaiah 51:2-3*

To journey through the Valley of Jezreel is to experience a marvellous transformation from mosquito ridden swamps to well cultivated land.

And yet an even more glorious future awaits the Jewish people:

> *"'The days are coming,' declares the Lord, 'when the reaper will be overtaken by the ploughman and the planter by the one treading grapes. New wine will drip from the mountains and flow from all the hills. I will bring back my exiled people Israel; they will rebuild the ruined cities and live in them. They will plant vineyards and drink their wine; they will make gardens and eat their fruit. I will plant Israel in their own land, never again to be uprooted from the land I have given them,' says the Lord your God."*
>
> Amos 9:13-15

As we know the Jewish people have been scattered over the face of the earth. Was this in God's plan? Indeed so! Listen again to the voice the prophets:

> *"Though I scatter them among the peoples, yet in distant lands they will remember me. They and their children will survive, and they will return."*
>
> Zechariah 10:9

On one occasion the disciples ask the Lord,

> *"Lord, are you at this time going to restore the kingdom to Israel?"*
> *Acts 1:6*

This was either a very foolish question or one that expressed the longing of every Jewish heart. There were a number of facts which the disciples took for granted in this question namely; that there once was a kingdom which was lost. Also that this kingdom would be restored and that Jesus, as Messiah, was the one to do it. What they wanted to know was would He do it at this visit or on His next visit.

If it was a foolish question Jesus would have said so, but he doesn't. Instead he says to them:

> *"It is not for you to know the times or dates the Father has set by his authority."*
> *Acts 1:7*

The implication in his answer is that it will happen sometime in the future.

Over this future kingdom the Lord himself will reign. The beautiful words of the prophets ring out:

> *"Of the increase of his government and peace there will be no end. He will reign on David's throne and over his kingdom, establishing*

and upholding it with justice and righteousness from that time on and for ever. The zeal of the Lord Almighty will accomplish this."

Isaiah 9:7

"In that day the Root of Jesse will stand as a banner for the peoples; the nations will rally to him and his place of rest will be glorious . . ."

Isaiah 11:10

Yes in God's eternal plan He has blinded the eyes of the Jewish people until the full number of Gentiles has been gathered in. Israel has experienced a hardening or blindness until the appointed time. A picture of this blindness is seen when Saul who was renamed Paul was blinded on the Damascus road. The Lord spoke to him and later in Damascus we read that the scales fell off his eyes. He could see! In the same way one day the last Gentile will be saved and the Lord will reveal himself to the Jewish people:

"I will pour out on the house of David and the inhabitants of Jerusalem a spirit of grace and supplication. They will look on the one they pierced, and they will mourn for him as one mourns for an only child."

Zechariah 12:10

> *"This is my covenant with them when*
> *I take away their sins."*
>
> *Romans 11:27*

What a debt we owe to the Jewish people. Christianity looks to Judaism for its roots. Judaism does not have to look to Christianity for its roots. We have been grafted in only because the Jewish branches were broken off—we Gentiles are the wild olive branches. Because of this we enjoy the blessings of Abraham through and by the grace of God.

Yes God still has plans for Israel and we are privileged to witness fulfilment of prophecy in our day. In a coming day Israel will be gloriously saved and the world will see that God keeps his promises.

Lest, however, we get impatient, listen again:

> *"Do not forget this one thing, dear*
> *friends: With the Lord a day is like*
> *a thousand years, and a thousand*
> *years are like a day. The Lord is not*
> *slow in keeping his promise, as some*
> *understand slowness. He is patient*
> *with you, not wanting anyone to*
> *perish, but everyone to come to*
> *repentance."*
>
> *2 Peter 3:8-9*

Let us therefore take a few moments to consider our own position before an almighty God who so loved us that he entered our scene to bear the punishment due to us.

CHAPTER 7

Blessings or Curses?

The noise of the horse's hooves clattering down the narrow pathway echoed around the gorge. The limestone walls on either side of the track went endlessly upwards and only let in a small amount of sunlight. The colours in the walls seemed to change as we rounded each corner. This was the fulfilment of one of my childhood dreams for as a lad my life's ambition was to visit Israel and then Petra. Here I was, walking down the Siq Gorge which was the entrance to the rose red city. Our guide stopped occasionally to point out interesting facts but I was impatient and wanted to go ahead into the city which I had looked forward to for so long. Suddenly we saw it. Illuminated by the strong sun—the Treasury—at the end of the narrow gorge, glowing pink against the darkness of the gorge—how amazing!

The whole edifice had been carved out of the solid rock face over 2000 years ago. We wandered round the extensive city marvelling at the many buildings, tombs, theatre and the rest. I climbed the many stairs to the high place. Each step had been chiselled out of the rock. Why had they gone to such lengths? At the top there was a flat area where sacrifices had been offered long ago. Offered to gods who could not hear or speak.

I sat and pondered for my view took in the whole city. Yes it was a magnificent city but there was one thing wrong. It was a dead city. There was no life! Plenty of tourists, plenty of peddlers selling their trinkets but no-one lived there. Why? What had happened? Well despite what the guide book said I knew something they were perhaps unwilling to recognise. The city was cursed. Petra was the centre of the Edomite peoples—it was called Bozrah. They were descendants of Esau and were a constant thorn in Israel's side. Prophets had repeatedly warned what was going to happen but all to no avail. Obadiah devoted all of his prophecy against Edom whilst Isaiah did not miss the mark:—

> *"God will stretch out over Edom the measuring line of chaos and the plumb-line of desolation."*
>
> *Isaiah 34:11*

It was none other than our Lord who cursed three towns in Israel. Chorazin, Capernaum and Bethsaida and today all we see are ruins. Woe to the man or woman who ignores the warnings of God.

We began by looking at the promises of God and how much we value and appreciate them. We continued by understanding that God never has to go back on his word. He is alpha and omega the beginning and the end. He sees tomorrow as though it had already happened.

Included in the promise to Abraham were these words:

> *"I will bless those who bless you, and whoever curses you I will curse . . ."*
> *Genesis 12:3*

When Mary gave thanks and glorified the Lord for the forthcoming birth of the Messiah, she said:

> *"He has helped his servant Israel, remembering to be merciful to Abraham and his descendants for ever, even as he said to our fathers."*
> *Luke 1:54-55*

This was to be the greatest blessing the world would ever experience—the coming of the anointed one; The Son of God; the Messiah; The Lamb of God who would be sacrificed for our sins.

Similarly when Zechariah prophesied under the guidance of the Holy Spirit he said:

> *"He has raised up a horn of salvation for us—to show mercy to our fathers and to remember his holy covenant, the oath he swore to our father Abraham; to rescue us from the hand of our enemies, and to enable us to*

> *serve him without fear in holiness*
> *and righteousness before him all our*
> *days."*
>
> Luke 1:69-75

God's promise was still remembered. In fact it is brought to mind throughout the scriptures.

There are many, no doubt, who will support and encourage Israel simply because of this promise that the Lord will bless those who bless Israel, and surely the Lord will indeed bless them for so doing. This, however, is a rather mercenary attitude and I do not think that this is a correct motive to employ. It is akin to serving the Lord for the heavenly rewards that we will one day receive.

Listen to what Paul has to say on the subject:

> *"For if the Gentiles have shared in*
> *the Jews' spiritual blessings, they owe*
> *it to the Jews to share with them their*
> *material blessings."*
>
> Romans 15:27

Surely we serve the Lord out of thankful and grateful hearts, recognising that we owe him our very lives. That we are not our own, we have been bought with a price—the precious blood of our Saviour Jesus Christ. In the same way we should support Israel by our prayers and deeds of kindness.

It was from the Jews that we received our scriptures. It was from converted Jews that the message of salvation was brought to the Gentile world. It is for the Jews that our Lord will return and stand again upon the Mount of Olives in Jerusalem.

History records that the Jews have suffered greatly at the hands of so called Christians and it is little wonder that believers in Jesus Christ in Israel today are known as Messianic Believers rather than Christians. As Christians we have nothing to be proud of as we look back over the centuries.

So have we been blessed spiritually? To answer this, first answer the question: Do I have faith?

If you have, then you have been and are still being blessed. Here is the authority:

> *"The scripture foresaw that God would justify the Gentiles by faith, and announced the gospel in advance to Abraham: 'All nations will be blessed through you.' So those who have faith are blessed along with Abraham the man of faith."*
>
> *Galatians 3:8*

Have you ever asked yourself why God redeemed you? Why did God love me so much that he was prepared and willing to suffer and die in such a cruel and tortuous manner? Here is the answer:

> *"He redeemed us in order that the blessing given to Abraham might come to the Gentiles through Christ Jesus, so that by faith we might receive the promise of the Spirit."*
>
> *Galatians 3:14*

Just how amazing is that? Our Lord wants to bless us with the same blessing that he gave to Abraham! How sad therefore that so many do not accept that this promise is everlasting and still applies today. They believe that it has been rescinded by God and despite the many times scripture confirms its current validity, they have no interest in it.

Paul continues this theme when writing to the Roman believers. He explains that Abraham received the promise before he was circumcised and therefore:

> *"he is the father of all who believe but have not been circumcised, in order that righteousness may be credited to them."*
>
> *Romans 4:11*

This blessing is not something that we can achieve by our own merit or something that can be attained by our own work. It is purely by faith in the living God. Surely the blessing referred to here must be in part none other than our salvation.

> *"For it is by grace you have been saved, through faith—and not from yourselves, it is the gift of God—not by works, so that no-one can boast."*
>
> *Ephesians 2:8-9*

Similarly Paul says to the Roman believers:

> *"For if those who live by the law are heirs, faith has no value and the*

promise is worthless, because the law brings wrath. And where there is no law there is no transgression. Therefore, the promise comes by faith, so that it may be by grace and may be guaranteed to all Abraham's offspring—not only to those who are of the law but also to those who are of faith in Abraham. He is the father of us all. As it is written: 'I have made you a father of many nations.'"

Romans 4:14-17

So it is, that all, whether Jew or Gentile, who have faith in Christ Jesus, are counted as heirs of Abraham and thus can revel in the blessings of our Father God which are given freely by his grace.

How wonderful that the promises which God made to Abraham can become ours. This was the purpose of our Lord's incarnation:

"For I tell you that Christ has become a servant of the Jews on behalf of God's truth, to confirm the promises made to the patriarchs so that the Gentiles may glorify God for his mercy, as it is written: 'Therefore I will praise you among the Gentiles; I will sing hymns to your name."

Romans 15:8-9

So then, we Gentiles, apart from God's promises to Abraham, have we anything to lay hold of? Are there no promises that are ours by right? Sorry—not one!

> *"Therefore, remember that formerly you who are Gentiles by birth and called uncircumcised by those who call themselves the circumcision (that done in the body by the hands of men)—remember that at that time you were separate from Christ, excluded from citizenship in Israel and foreigners to the covenants of the promise, without hope and without God in the world. But now in Christ Jesus you who once were far away have been brought near through the blood of Christ."*
>
> *Ephesians 2:11-12*

We were excluded and foreigners to the covenants of promise but now have been brought near.

Don't just sit there! Shout Hallelujah!

Wait a moment. Before we start doing cartwheels there is a flip side. Let us have another look at that verse:

> *"I will bless those who bless you, and whoever curses you I will curse . . ."*
>
> *Genesis 12:3*

Do you notice that the first half of the verse about blessings is plural? 'Those who bless you.'

The second half of the verse is singular. 'Whoever curses you.' The authorised version puts it this way: 'and curse him that curseth thee.'

This involves you and me as individuals having to make up our own minds about where we stand in relation to Israel and God's promises to them. We cannot hide behind an organisation to which we subscribe or even to a church denomination. We will be held accountable for our own actions.

So what are these curses? I cannot say, but some examples of curses which God promises to the Israelites if they disobeyed can be perused in Deuteronomy 28.

Today we are living in a world where the Word of God is no longer respected. Laws are passed which conflict with scripture and to be a Christian is increasingly becoming an object of ridicule if not persecution. The Word of God is the handbook for our daily living. Through the scriptures our heavenly father speaks to us and we delight in his many promises to us.

Once we start to ignore or discount sections of his word we are on a slippery slope.

God refers to Israel as his treasured possession. If the Spirit of Christ is within us then that should be our passion too.

Many sections of the Church today ignore Israel and the Jewish people. Prophesies concerning future events mean nothing and are seldom if ever taught.

> *"Do not be arrogant, but be afraid.*
> *For if God did not spare the natural*
> *branches, he will not spare you*
> *either."*
>
> *Romans 11:20-21*

At the outset I mentioned a promise given to my brother and me by my father which we did not particular want to receive. It involved punishment!

God here is giving us a choice. We can receive his blessing or his wrath.

It behoves us therefore to examine our thoughts and deeds towards Israel in the light of scripture in order that we might be in a right relationship with our heavenly father.